About this book

Have you ever noticed? how quickly you react before you've had time to think?

Why certain patterns repeat, even when you know better?

Why some decisions feel deliberate, while others feel automatic?

Why effort doesn't always lead to change — and insight doesn't always lead to control?

At what point does a thought become an action?

Where does an impulse actually come from? And if so much of our behavior seems to arrive before we are aware of it...

what does it really mean to choose? Pause does not tell you what to believe. It begins with a quieter inquiry:

what unfolds between impulse and action?

Drawing from psychology, neuroscience, and lived experience, this book explores how emotion, habit, memory, and unconscious preparation shape behavior long before intention appears — and why awareness often arrives after a direction is already forming. This book does not argue against agency. It examines where participation becomes possible, and how presence can alter what would otherwise move unchecked.

PAUSE.

What Happens Between Impulse and Action

Koushik Gaja

First published in 2025

Independently published.

Table of Contents

Author's Note

This book is not written to persuade, instruct, or reassure.

It is written to be followed.

Much of what is explored here unfolds beneath deliberate awareness—through emotional momentum, habitual response, cognitive framing, and unconscious preparation. Because of this, the book is best read slowly, without searching for conclusions too early. Many of its observations are not meant to be accepted or rejected immediately, but noticed against lived experience.

The language used here is intentional. Terms such as choice, agency, awareness, and responsibility are not used in their everyday sense, nor as fixed philosophical positions. Their meaning develops gradually through the progression of the inquiry itself. Early chapters describe how responses form before reflection. Later chapters clarify where participation becomes possible once that formation is seen.

This is not a guide offering techniques, guarantees, or optimization strategies. It does not promise control, mastery, or resolution. Nor is it a purely academic work. While it draws from psychology and neuroscience where relevant, its focus remains practical and experiential: how action actually takes shape moment to moment.

Some readers may experience discomfort, uncertainty, or resistance while reading. These responses are not obstacles. They often indicate that familiar ways of interpreting action and responsibility are being interrupted.

If there is a single instruction for reading this book, it is this:

Do not rush to decide what it means.

Stay with what is being described long enough to recognize it.

Preface

For a long time, I moved through my days assuming I was deciding as I went.

I spoke, reacted, agreed, withdrew, committed, and changed direction with the quiet confidence that these movements were mine. They felt immediate, natural, and justified. I rarely questioned where they came from. I only noticed their consequences.

Over time, something subtle began to bother me.

I started noticing how often my reactions arrived before my thoughts. How familiar situations pulled familiar responses out of me, even when I believed I had outgrown them. How insight didn't always change behavior, and intention didn't always translate into action.

The question that stayed with me was not dramatic. It was simple, and persistent:

Why does this keep happening?

That question didn't lead to answers right away. It led to observation. To slowing down moments that usually passed too quickly. To paying attention not just to what I did, but to how responses formed before I could name them.

This book grew out of that attention.

It is not a record of conclusions. It is a record of noticing. Of watching reactions assemble themselves. Of seeing how often action was already leaning in a direction by the time I felt involved.

Nothing here began as theory. It began as experience – repeated, uncomfortable, ordinary experience.

If there is anything I hope this book offers, it is not certainty, reassurance, or instruction. It is recognition. The kind that happens when something you've felt but never quite named starts to become visible.

This is not an invitation to fix yourself.

It is an invitation to pause.

Koushik Gaja

Introduction

Most of us move through life believing we choose our paths with intention. We imagine ourselves standing at the center of our decisions, evaluating possibilities, weighing consequences, and ultimately selecting our actions from a place of conscious authority. This is the story we tell ourselves—one of autonomy, direction, and deliberate control.

But if we slow down enough to observe our inner movements, that story begins to strain.

We notice how instinctively we react to discomfort, how quickly we fall into familiar patterns, and how often our emotions shape our responses long before reasoning appears. We notice how the same habits repeat across years, how we justify actions after they happen, and how certain "decisions" feel more like automatic responses than deliberate ones.

The truth is less flattering but more precise: much of what we experience as deciding is driven by momentum.

Momentum from childhood conditions.

Momentum from emotional reflexes.

Momentum from learned behavior.

Momentum from beliefs we never examined.

We inherit tendencies without noticing.

We follow impulses without questioning.

We move toward what feels familiar, and only later claim it was intentional.

This book begins at that uncomfortable threshold—the point where action no longer appears to begin where we thought it did. This is not an attempt to weaken responsibility, but to locate it more accurately. Because if our actions are shaped by forces we do not see, then understanding those forces becomes the first step toward meaningful participation in how we act.

Here, we will explore the internal architecture that guides human behavior: the emotional circuits that prepare our reactions, the cognitive patterns that filter perception, and the unconscious mechanisms that shape responses before conscious intention fully forms. These processes are not flaws in the human mind; they are its foundations. But foundations can limit or support us depending on whether we understand them.

Recognizing the limits of conscious control is not an act of surrender.

It is the beginning of precision.

Responsiveness is not the absence of influence; it is awareness of influence. It is the gradual process of seeing what shapes us so that reaction is not the only possible outcome. The more clearly we understand the forces moving within us, the more capable we become of participating in how our actions unfold.

This book does not attempt to dismantle hope or deny possibility. It seeks to illuminate the quiet mechanisms that govern behavior so we can step out of automatic repetition —and into a more deliberate relationship with what moves us.

Understanding begins here:

with the simple, difficult question of where our actions actually begin.

If action often feels automatic, the natural question is: where does that momentum come from?

This book advances a careful claim.

Agency does not begin at the origin of impulse, but in the capacity to remain present as movement is forming. What we experience as choosing is rarely creation from nothing; it is participation within momentum shaped by inheritance, emotion, cognition, and habit.

What follows is not a guide to mastery, nor an argument for despair. It is an inquiry into where influence actually operates once automaticity is seen clearly. By the end of this book, the reader should be able to—

- recognize how emotional and cognitive momentum prepares action before awareness fully arrives

- distinguish between impulse, interpretation, and execution as distinct phases rather than a single event

- see how habits stabilize through repetition beneath awareness

- locate the narrow interval where participation becomes possible, even when control is limited

- understand responsibility not as command over impulse, but as influence over patterns across time

Scope and Limits

This book does not attempt to resolve every debate surrounding agency, responsibility, or moral judgment. Its aim is narrower and more practical: to examine how action unfolds in lived experience, and where meaningful participation becomes functionally available within that process.

The scientific findings discussed here do not claim to describe all forms of decision-making, nor to eliminate planning, deliberation, or reflection. Rather, they illuminate the conditions under which unconscious preparation, emotional momentum, and cognitive framing shape what becomes available to awareness.

Philosophical accounts that emphasize rational control or reasons-based action are not rejected here, but bracketed. This book asks a prior question: what must already be in place, internally, for those forms of agency to operate at all?

Chapter 1

Before Intention

We like to believe that choice begins the moment we become aware of it. We imagine ourselves standing at the center of each decision, weighing options, examining consequences, and deliberately selecting the path that best aligns with our values. This picture feels intuitive, comforting, almost noble. It is the story we tell ourselves about how the mind works: that intention precedes action, that awareness guides behavior, and that we are, at our core, rational beings shaping our own lives through conscious will.

But beneath this familiar story lies a different reality—one that psychology, neuroscience, and simple observation have been revealing for decades. Much of what we call "choice" is shaped long before consciousness arrives. The surface of decision-making may feel deliberate, but the undercurrent is anything but.

Consider how often we "decide" quickly: choosing between two similar items at a store, responding to a message, selecting a seat in a room, or picking a route home. These moments feel light and effortless, as if the mind is performing a simple act of reasoning. Yet research shows that subtle, unnoticed influences—colors, framing, mood, recent memories, ease of processing—shape our preferences before rational analysis even begins. Kahneman's work in Thinking, Fast and Slow (2011) made this clear: our minds run two systems, one fast and intuitive, the other slow and deliberate, and the fast system often prepares the path long before the slow one appears.

You can feel this most clearly in moments that seem too small to matter. You reply to a message and only afterward realize the tone you used, or you click "buy" and then wonder why that option felt right without knowing exactly why.

And it is here, in the quiet gap between impulse and awareness, that one of the most important findings in the science of free will appears. Benjamin Libet's work in 1983 made this clearer than any theory could. In his experiment, the brain began preparing an action several hundred milliseconds before the person reported the conscious intention to act. The impulse to move did not originate in awareness; it appeared in neural activity beneath it. Conscious intention arrived late, stepping into a process already underway. Libet's findings forced a reversal in the story we tell about ourselves: the brain moves first, and the self joins afterward. Awareness does not initiate choice as much as it interprets it. Later work has debated what exactly this neural activity represents. Some researchers suggest it reflects a gradual buildup of readiness rather than a completed decision. But regardless of interpretation, the central insight remains: the machinery of action begins organizing itself before intention is consciously felt.

This does not mean that a hidden decision has already been made in full, or that conscious intention is irrelevant. What these findings consistently show is more limited and more important: neural preparation precedes awareness of intention. By the time intention is felt, the system is already in motion, even if its eventual outcome is not yet fixed.

This doesn't make the mind defective. It simply reveals that the architecture of choice is more intricate than the story of rational autonomy allows. The brain evolved to handle complexity quickly, often through shortcuts—heuristics that operate beneath awareness. These shortcuts allow us to navigate daily life without drowning in analysis, but they also mean that the origins of many decisions are hidden from us.

What we experience as deciding often coincides with the moment awareness arrives, not the moment preparation begins.

Even moments that appear intentional are frequently driven by emotional signals that arise before we consciously detect them. Emotional responses are not the intruders we treat them as; they are the ground on which cognitive judgment stands. Robert Zajonc's research on affective primacy showed that emotional reactions occur milliseconds before the brain generates a conscious interpretation. Fear tightens our attention, excitement expands it, uncertainty makes familiar options feel safer, and even slight discomfort can steer us away from a choice that reason might support.

We rarely acknowledge this, not because we deny emotion, but because emotion does not announce itself. It moves beneath language. It colors experience rather than appearing within it.

And it is not only emotion that shapes us. Social forces form another layer beneath what we call choice. Humans are profoundly social creatures; belonging and recognition influence far more decisions than we admit. A career path may feel chosen because it "suits us," when in truth it suits the expectations of those whose approval we fear losing. A purchase might reflect personal taste, but it may also reflect a desire to signal identity, status, or competence. Cultural norms seep so deeply into our thinking that we mistake them for personal preference. We feel as though we are choosing freely, but we are often choosing from within a narrow range of what our environment has made familiar.

Then there is intuition—the quick, confident sense of what to do. We trust it because it arrives fully formed. Psychology describes intuition not as magic but as rapid pattern recognition. It can be remarkably accurate when rooted in experience, and deeply flawed when rooted in bias. Intuition draws on what we have lived before, but it also draws on what we have avoided, what we fear, and what we have normalized. It is neither an enemy nor a guide —it is a mirror, revealing our accumulated patterns without explaining them.

And layered over all of this is the simple fact that the mind's resources are limited. Decision fatigue—demonstrated in research by Baumeister and colleagues (1998)—shows that the more decisions we make, the more the mind gravitates toward the easiest available option. Not the best option, not the wisest one, but the one requiring the least cognitive effort. At the end of a long day, the mind chooses relief, not logic. In these moments, we are not exercising autonomy as much as surrendering to exhaustion. Choice becomes a matter of conserving energy, not expressing intention.

When we step back and observe these forces together, a different picture of choice begins to emerge.

Emotion often moves first, setting the tone before thought appears. Intuition shapes judgment by drawing on patterns we may not recognize. Social norms quietly narrow what feels acceptable or possible. Cognitive shortcuts fill in gaps where attention runs thin. Fatigue weakens deliberation, pushing the mind toward ease rather than evaluation.

Think of a familiar situation: a conversation that turns sharp, a late-night decision made when energy is low, or agreeing to something you did not want because refusing felt harder. In those moments, nothing feels forced, yet everything feels guided. The response feels like "you," even as it unfolds faster than reflection can catch.

Seen individually, these influences feel minor. Seen together, they form a continuous chain. Choice no longer appears as a single, clear moment, but as the endpoint of processes already in motion.

Conscious reasoning still participates in this chain. But it does not always initiate it. Often, it arrives late and takes credit for decisions that were already unfolding.

This view may seem unsettling at first, because it challenges the assumption that we are the exclusive authors of our actions. But recognizing the limits of conscious choice does not diminish our humanity. It reveals its depth. The mind is not a spotlight shining neatly on options; it is a layered organism shaped by a lifetime of experiences, instincts, memories, emotions, and cultural imprints. To understand this is not to lose freedom but to locate it correctly.

Choice does not begin at the moment of awareness.

It begins in the silent processes beneath it.

Freedom becomes possible when these influences are seen before they complete themselves.

Only when we understand what moves us can we begin to move differently.

Only when we see the machinery beneath the surface can we shape the direction it takes.

What we experience as choosing often begins earlier than we notice. By the time intention becomes clear, processes of orientation, preference, and readiness are already active.

This chapter does not question whether we choose. It examines when choosing becomes possible.

Real autonomy begins much earlier, in the quiet architecture of the mind.

The task is not to escape this architecture, but to become aware of it.

Awareness is the first act of freedom.

If choice begins beneath awareness, the next question is obvious: what is the origin of that deeper layer? We turn now to the forces that build the mind before we know it.

Chapter 2

The Inherited Mind

The mind we carry into adulthood often feels self-created, the product of our reflections, choices, and experiences. But much of its structure predates our awareness. Before we ever think about who we are, the world has already begun shaping us. Long before we form beliefs, we inherit tendencies; long before we reason, we absorb patterns; long before we question, we imitate. Our earliest lessons are not deliberate, and our earliest influences are not chosen. They form the quiet architecture beneath the self we claim as our own.

You can sense this inheritance most clearly when you react before you know why. When something feels immediately comforting or immediately threatening, even though you cannot explain it. When a tone of voice unsettles you, or silence feels heavy, or closeness feels either natural or overwhelming without any obvious reason. These reactions do not arrive with explanations. They arrive already formed.

Some inheritance is biological. Research in behavioral genetics, including the work of Thomas and Chess (1977), suggests that temperament—our baseline emotional style—

appears early in life. One child startles easily; another is unbothered by noise. One seeks novelty; another clings to familiarity. These are not choices; they are inclinations, emotional settings through which the world first filters. They do not define us, but they create the contours through which experience will later flow.

Yet temperament alone does not shape the mind. The emotional environment around us begins weaving its own threads long before we can understand them. Attachment theory shows how early interactions form patterns that echo throughout life. A caregiver's responsiveness teaches a child whether the world is predictable or unpredictable, safe or unsafe, open or closed. These lessons are not taught through explanation. They are learned through rhythm—the rhythm of being held or not, soothed or not, heard or not. These early impressions become internal templates for trust, fear, closeness, and retreat. They do not feel like lessons because they are older than memory.

Consider how differently people respond to the same situation. One person reads a delayed reply as harmless; another feels an immediate pull toward anxiety or rejection. One person interprets raised voices as danger; another barely notices. These differences are rarely about logic. They are echoes of emotional climates learned before reasoning existed.

As language enters, it brings not only words but emotional tone. A phrase spoken in calm reassurance carries a different weight than the same phrase spoken with irritation. Over years, these subtleties accumulate, forming habits of self-talk we rarely notice. The voice inside us is built partly from the voices that surrounded us. How we admonish ourselves, how we forgive, how we doubt, how we push — these patterns are stitched together from years of listening to how others spoke to us and around us.

As we grow, our inheritance expands into the social world. We observe not only what people say, but how they behave—how they handle conflict, how they treat uncertainty, how they react to difference. We learn approval and shame long before we understand them. We absorb what is admired, what is mocked, what is forbidden, what is rewarded. These are not explicit teachings but quiet transmissions. A child watches a parent suppress an emotion and learns what must be hidden; watches them raise their voice and learns what is permitted; watches them avoid discomfort and learns the same pattern without ever being told.

Culture then adds its own shaping force. Every society has unstated rules—what constitutes respect, what success looks like, which emotions are acceptable, which dreams are realistic. Moral intuitions emerge not from personal reflection alone but from the shared emotional narratives of the group. What feels "normal" or "right" is often an absorption of cultural rhythm rather than a product of individual choice. We mistake familiarity for preference, and internalized norms for personal identity.

By the time we reach adolescence, the inheritance is already vast. We carry predispositions we did not choose, emotional patterns formed before memory, communication habits shaped by environment, social rules absorbed through observation, and cultural frameworks that feel like our own viewpoints. These forces operate quietly, creating the scaffolding on which identity later forms. They influence our desires, fears, comforts, and aversions — not forcefully, but subtly, in the way a landscape shapes the path a river takes.

When we finally reach the point of conscious reflection, we encounter a mind already furnished. We think we are shaping ourselves from scratch, but we are mostly rearranging what was placed there long before awareness developed. This is not a limitation but a truth. The self is not an invention; it is an inheritance gradually made conscious.

To recognize this inheritance is not to reject it. It is to understand that the mind is not neutral ground. It is a structure shaped by countless forces — biological, emotional, social, cultural — long before it becomes self-aware. And because these forces acted before we could choose them, they often feel invisible. Their influence appears as instinct, preference, personality, or intuition, when in fact they are the sediment of experiences and patterns absorbed before we ever asked who we wanted to become.

The more closely we examine this inherited structure, the clearer it becomes that we learned how to feel long before we learned how to think. A child does not first understand the world through concepts but through sensations: safety and danger, closeness and distance, acceptance and dismissal. These sensations form emotional grooves. With time, those grooves become patterns, and those patterns begin to feel like the natural movement of the self. By adulthood, these early emotional pathways can be so familiar that they appear to be part of personality rather than part of history.

This is why some people find it easier to trust while others default to caution; why some instinctively seek connection and others instinctively guard against it; why certain individuals interpret silence as peace while others interpret it as rejection. These are not abstract personal choices. They are shaped by the terrains we traversed before we had the language to explain them.

Cognitive inheritance follows a similar path. We absorb not only emotional cues but patterns of attention and interpretation. A child whose curiosity is welcomed learns to look outward with interest; a child whose questions are dismissed learns to turn inward and stay silent. A child raised where mistakes are met with patience learns that errors are part of growth; a child punished for the same mistakes learns that failure is dangerous. These lessons become internal frameworks through which the world is interpreted. We notice what we have been trained to notice, avoid what we have been taught to fear, and overlook what was never pointed out to us.

Even our sense of identity—what kind of person we believe ourselves to be—is rooted in early mirrors. We first see ourselves reflected in the reactions of others: pride, irritation, affection, disappointment. If those reflections were consistent, we formed a stable sense of self; if they were erratic, we learned to adapt, perform, or withdraw. Identity begins not as an act of self-authoring but as an interpretation of the emotional responses we received. We construct ourselves from how others responded to us long before we consciously choose who we wish to be.

Many adults spend years trying to change what feels like "who they are," without realizing they are responding to roles learned early. The responsible one. The difficult one. The quiet one. The reliable one. These identities often began as adaptations, not choices — ways of staying safe, accepted, or unseen.

These patterns rarely feel inherited because they do not speak in the language of memory. They speak in the language of familiarity. What is familiar feels true; what is habitual feels natural; what is inherited feels personal. And so the mind built before awareness becomes the mind we experience as "me." The inheritance becomes indistinguishable from identity.

None of this implies that the self is fixed or predetermined. It simply means that the starting point of our self-awareness is built on a foundation we did not lay. We wake up midway through the construction of our inner world, and only then begin to make sense of the architecture around us. It is like arriving late to a story already in progress: we interpret the plot as if we had been present from the first page, unaware of the unseen chapters that shape the meaning of everything that follows.

By the time we make our first "independent" decision, the psychological machinery behind that decision has been forming for years.

We filter possibilities through inherited emotional patterns, evaluate risks through inherited fears, and interpret situations through inherited beliefs. We feel as though we are making isolated choices, but in truth, we are moving through pathways carved long before we had the ability to question them.

This realization can feel uncomfortable.

This does not diminish agency—it defines its boundaries. Real autonomy begins not in denying what shaped us, but in recognizing it. The inherited mind is not an obstacle to freedom. It is the starting point from which freedom must be built.

Most people never examine the mind they inherited. They simply use it, assuming that its reactions, preferences, and tendencies are expressions of their true self. But a mind unexamined becomes a mind unquestioned, and a mind unquestioned becomes a mind repeated. The deeper we look into our inheritance, the clearer it becomes that many of our "selves" are personas constructed to adapt to early environments.

To become conscious of this inheritance is not to reject it, but to finally see it. Awareness turns the implicit into the explicit, the automatic into the intentional, the background into the foreground. When we recognize the forces that shaped us, we become capable of responding to them rather than being quietly directed by them.

The mind we inherit does not determine who we must become. It determines the terrain on which we begin. Freedom, if it is to mean anything, must begin with understanding the soil in which we were planted. Only then can we decide how to grow beyond it.

As we look more closely, a deeper truth emerges:

the mind does not merely inherit emotional and cognitive patterns — it inherits momentum. Emotional reflexes formed in childhood continue into adulthood, shaping how we respond before we have the chance to think. These reflexes are so immediate and so consistent that they often feel like part of our nature. But they are not nature alone. They are conditioned responses—patterns repeated until they become automatic.

And this brings us to the next layer of the mind's architecture. If inheritance forms the structure, emotion provides the energy. To understand why our choices feel constrained, we must understand the emotional forces that activate before awareness—the ones that rise beneath thought and guide us without requesting permission. These forces are not abstract; they have weight, direction, urgency. They create impulses, aversions, and attractions that give the inherited mind its movement.

Chapter 3

Emotional Momentum

Emotion often moves before thought. Not always, and not in every situation, but in many of the subtle internal shifts that shape daily experience. Before we interpret an event or form a deliberate response, emotion has already begun to influence the direction in which the mind will move. It does this quietly, as a shift in attention or posture, long before awareness begins to explain what is happening.

We often imagine that reasoning leads our decisions, and emotion follows. But psychological and neuroscientific work suggests a more layered sequence. Researchers like Joseph LeDoux have shown that emotional pathways in the brain can activate before the systems responsible for deliberate reflection have time to respond. A facial expression, a tone, a sudden sound—all can trigger emotional activation in milliseconds. This early movement is not interpretation; it is orientation.

After this initial reaction, emotion begins shaping how the world is perceived. It draws attention toward certain details and away from others. A slight unease can make neutral expressions feel pointed; calmness can make ambiguity feel harmless. Robert Zajonc's work on affective primacy suggests that emotional evaluations can occur before conscious judgment, giving experience a subtle tilt before thought has formed a position. What we notice and what we ignore, what seems meaningful and what seems irrelevant, are influenced by this emotional orientation long before we recognize it.

Only after these early movements does conscious interpretation begin. Kahneman's dual-process model describes this as the slower system of thought joining a process already in motion, refining or justifying the emotional draft that came before it. We do not begin our reasoning from a neutral point. We begin from a state already shaped by emotional activation and by the tendencies we inherited from earlier experiences. Thought enters as an organizer, not an initiator.

None of this implies that emotion overwhelms reason or that reflection becomes impossible. It only clarifies the order in which mental processes often unfold. Emotion supplies the first movement, the first shift in direction. Thought follows within that movement, sometimes supporting it, sometimes questioning it, but rarely preceding it. The two are connected, not opposed.

These emotional movements do not arise in isolation. They are shaped by layers of inheritance and learning that precede conscious awareness. Some of these layers are biological. The human nervous system carries tendencies that reflect long histories of adaptation—sensitivities to threat, attraction to safety, responsiveness to novelty, and aversion to uncertainty. These tendencies are not specific emotions, but predispositions: ways in which the body is prepared to respond before experience adds detail.

Over time, experience begins to refine these predispositions. Repeated exposure to certain conditions strengthens some responses and weakens others. Situations that are consistently followed by safety, reward, or relief tend to produce calm and openness; situations followed by discomfort or uncertainty tend to produce tension and vigilance. Through repetition, the body learns patterns before the mind learns explanations. These patterns do not feel learned because they are absorbed gradually, through experience rather than instruction.

Emotion, in this sense, functions less as a spontaneous reaction and more as a form of stored adaptation. This does not mean emotion is irrational or something to be eliminated; it means it is faster than explanation. It is accumulated information—biological, experiential, and contextual—expressing itself through bodily response in the present moment. What appears as impulse is often the body applying past learning faster than conscious reflection can intervene. Emotion does not announce its origin. It presents itself as immediacy.

Childhood plays a significant role in this process, not because it is the only formative period, but because it is where repetition is most frequent and awareness is least developed. Early environments provide consistent patterns to which the nervous system adapts. A child repeatedly soothed learns one mode of response; a child repeatedly exposed to unpredictability learns another. Over time, these responses stabilize. They become familiar pathways that guide attention and shape interpretation long before conscious thought evaluates a situation.

By adulthood, these emotional patterns feel instinctive. They influence what feels possible, what feels threatening, and what feels significant before reasoning begins. Much of what is later described as intuition can be understood as emotional memory—patterns of response formed through inheritance and repetition, operating beneath awareness.

Emotion also shapes interpretation in ways that are often invisible. The same silence can feel peaceful to one person and uneasy to another. A delay in communication can be understood as patience or as rejection. These differences do not arise from the situations themselves, but from the emotional patterns through which they are perceived. Meaning forms around the emotional state already in place.

Think of a moment when a comment lingered longer than it should have.

Nothing overtly hostile was said, yet your body tightened. Attention narrowed. Meaning began forming before you could stop it. By the time you thought, Why did that bother me?, the emotional tone was already set.

If one pays attention closely, emotional movement can be noticed in the order it appears: the initial reaction in the body, the shift in attention, and the early formation of interpretation. Observing this sequence is not a technique but a way of seeing what is already taking place beneath awareness.

To see emotional determinism clearly is not to reduce the mind to reflex. It is to understand the architecture beneath our reactions. Emotion does not erase our ability to reason, but it creates the conditions in which reasoning occurs. It influences what rises to awareness, how quickly it arises, and in what emotional atmosphere it is received.

Recognizing this sequence does not diminish agency. Instead, it marks the point where agency begins. When emotional movements operate unnoticed, they guide behavior without our participation. When they become visible, even briefly, a space appears between impulse and action. It is small at first, but it can expand. Within this space, the possibility of deliberate choice emerges.

Emotion gives the inherited mind its momentum. Awareness determines whether that momentum becomes repetition or transformation. To understand this relationship is essential before turning to the next layer of the mind: the cognitive structures that interpret emotional signals and shape the forms our thinking takes.

Chapter 4

Cognitive Framing

If emotion provides the initial movement of the mind, cognition provides the structure through which that movement is shaped. Thought does not meet experience as a blank surface, nor does it begin from neutrality. By the time conscious reflection appears, experience has already been filtered, organized, and given form through cognitive processes operating beneath awareness.

We often imagine thinking as a deliberate act: a mind encountering the world, weighing information, and arriving at conclusions through reason. But much of cognition functions before deliberation has time to begin. It operates as a system of expectations and patterns that give experience coherence quickly, so that the world does not feel fragmented or overwhelming. What we later call "analysis" is often the refinement of an interpretation that has already begun to settle into place.

The first cognitive operation in this sequence is attention. At any given moment, the environment presents far more information than the mind can consciously register. Sounds overlap, visual details compete, internal sensations arise, memories surface, and possibilities multiply. Attention narrows this field. Certain elements are selected, while others fade into the background or disappear entirely. This narrowing does not feel like an act of choice. It feels like reality itself presenting what matters.

Yet what draws attention is not random. It is shaped by prior learning, emotional orientation, and familiarity. A person attuned to threat notices different details than someone attuned to opportunity. A mind trained by past experiences highlights some cues and disregards others before conscious awareness has time to intervene. Attention, in this sense, is guided long before it is chosen.

Once attention settles on a particular detail, interpretation follows. The mind begins assigning meaning to what has been selected. A tone of voice becomes reassuring or dismissive. A pause becomes calm or tense. A facial expression is read as curiosity, disapproval, or indifference. These interpretations do not announce themselves as assumptions. They feel immediate and self-evident, as though the meaning were inherent in the situation itself.

Interpretation draws heavily on patterns formed through repetition. When similar situations have led to similar outcomes in the past, the mind learns to associate certain cues with certain meanings. Over time, these associations become efficient. They arise quickly, require little effort, and feel reliable. Alternative interpretations remain possible, but they require more attention and energy to access. Familiar meanings take priority not because they are more accurate, but because they are easier to retrieve.

From interpretation emerges expectation. The mind does not only make sense of the present; it prepares for what it believes will happen next. This preparation is subtle. It may appear as a tightening of the body, a readiness to speak, a hesitation to act, or an inclination to withdraw. Expectation shapes posture, tone, and emotional readiness before any conscious plan is formed. In this way, cognition participates in shaping experience forward in time, not merely reacting to it.

As expectations are confirmed, they are reinforced. Interpretations that align with outcomes become more stable. They feel increasingly obvious, increasingly correct. When expectations are violated, revision becomes possible, but revision is slower and more demanding than reinforcement. It requires attention, openness, and often discomfort. As a result, cognitive patterns tend to stabilize rather than dissolve. Beliefs harden not because they are true, but because they have been repeated.

Over time, these stabilized interpretations begin to feel personal. They align with identity. Certain ways of seeing the world come to feel like expressions of "who I am." Contradictory interpretations may be dismissed not on evidential grounds, but because they threaten coherence. The mind resists disruption not out of stubbornness, but out of an implicit drive to maintain continuity. What feels like intellectual certainty is often the preservation of an established frame.

Emotion and cognition then reinforce one another. An interpretation of threat intensifies fear; fear sharpens attention toward confirming details. An interpretation of safety permits calm; calm broadens attention and softens interpretation. In this way, emotional activation strengthens cognitive framing, and cognitive framing stabilizes emotional response. The system becomes self-reinforcing. The mind moves along familiar pathways not because the situation demands it, but because the internal architecture has learned to do so.

Conscious reasoning enters this process later than we typically assume. Reflection can examine interpretations, question assumptions, and introduce alternative perspectives. But it does not begin from nothing. It works with material already shaped by attention, interpretation, and expectation. When we "think something through," we are often reorganizing what has already been prepared rather than initiating a fresh evaluation. Reason edits more than it authors.

This does not make reasoning irrelevant. It clarifies its limits. Cognition is not the origin of judgment, but the structure through which judgment becomes coherent. It allows experience to make sense, but it also constrains what can be seen easily. What we experience as freedom of thought is often the freedom to move within boundaries that were established without conscious participation.

Understanding cognitive determinism helps explain why certain beliefs feel compelling even when evidence is weak, why some ideas feel immediately implausible despite their logic, and why changing one's mind can feel disorienting or threatening. These reactions are not failures of intelligence. They reflect a system designed to preserve coherence and predictability before accuracy.

If cognition operates through inherited and conditioned structures, then intellectual autonomy cannot mean unrestricted freedom of thought. It must mean something more limited and more demanding: the capacity to notice how thinking is shaped, and to remain present long enough to introduce revision. This capacity does not arise through force of will alone. It requires sustained attention, repetition, and an openness to uncertainty.

Freedom, in this sense, does not emerge from escaping structure, but from becoming aware of it. A mind that cannot see its own interpretive habits experiences them as reality itself. A mind that begins to recognize those habits gains a narrow but meaningful margin of movement. Within that margin, interpretations can be softened, expectations questioned, and reactions redirected.

This margin is not wide, and it is not stable. It requires effort to maintain and tends to collapse under fatigue or stress. But it exists. Cognitive determinism does not eliminate agency; it defines the conditions under which agency becomes possible. Thought becomes freer not when it abandons its patterns, but when it learns to see them.

As emotional determinism provides momentum, cognitive determinism provides direction. Together, they explain why behavior feels both compelled and personal, automatic and meaningful. They also explain why insight alone rarely produces lasting change. Understanding the system does not dissolve it. Change requires something more concrete.

The next layer of this system concerns action itself—not the moments we imagine as choices, but the repeated behaviors through which emotional and cognitive patterns are expressed and reinforced. These behaviors form loops that stabilize internal dynamics and give them visible form. To understand how freedom might be constructed in practice, we must now examine how habit translates internal momentum into consistent action.

Chapter 5

Habits & Behavioural Loops

Behavior rarely appears as a series of isolated actions. It unfolds as patterns. What we do once is rarely what defines us; what we do repeatedly is. These repetitions do not arise because we consciously decide to repeat ourselves, but because internal momentum finds stable pathways through action.

A habit is not a flaw in character. It is a solution the mind has found to reduce effort. When emotional and cognitive processes align in a particular way, behavior becomes the outlet through which that alignment is expressed. Once a behavior successfully resolves tension, uncertainty, or desire, the mind remembers it. The next time a similar state arises, the same behavior is prepared again, often before awareness notices the cue.

This is how loops form.

A situation triggers an emotional response. That response activates a familiar interpretation. The interpretation inclines the body toward a particular action. The action produces an outcome—relief, stimulation, distraction, or control. If the outcome satisfies the underlying state, the loop is reinforced. Over time, the loop becomes faster and more automatic. What began as a response turns into a routine.

The critical feature of habit is not repetition alone, but invisibility. Once a loop stabilizes, it no longer feels like a sequence. It feels like a single impulse. The person does not experience "cue, reaction, interpretation, action." They experience "this is what I did." The steps collapse into immediacy.

What allows this collapse is familiarity. The mind favors responses that require the least negotiation. Known pathways feel safer than uncertain alternatives, even when those alternatives might be more aligned with present needs. Familiarity is mistaken for suitability. Efficiency is mistaken for intention.

Over time, these loops begin to shape expectation. Certain situations start to feel as though they require a particular response. The individual no longer asks what to do. Attention narrows, the body prepares, and behavior unfolds along a familiar path. Awareness may be present, but it is no longer decisive. It arrives late, often just in time to explain what has already occurred.

This is where habit stops feeling mechanical and starts feeling personal. Repeated behavior becomes evidence of self. The individual does not think, "I respond this way because a loop has formed." They think, "This is how I am." What began as adaptation is absorbed into identity. To behave differently now feels not merely difficult, but incongruent.

The strength of a habit does not depend on how often it repeats, but on how deeply it is justified. Behaviors reinforced by relief, approval, or moral meaning stabilize more quickly than those reinforced by pleasure alone. When a response is associated with being responsible, kind, disciplined, or good, questioning it feels unnecessary. The loop becomes protected by interpretation.

These justifications do not arise solely from within. They are often supplied and reinforced by the surrounding world. Families reward certain responses. Institutions normalize particular forms of compliance. Cultures elevate some behaviors to moral ideals while discouraging others as weakness or failure. Over time, external reinforcement becomes internal expectation. What is praised repeatedly begins to feel necessary. What feels necessary begins to feel chosen.

In this way, many habits are not merely personal patterns but adaptations to social environments. They persist not because the individual consciously endorses them, but because deviation carries cost—disapproval, exclusion, guilt, or instability. The loop survives because it is supported from both sides: internally by familiarity, and externally by reward.

This is why many patterns persist without resistance. They do not announce themselves as habits. They present themselves as values. The repetition is invisible because it aligns with what the individual has been taught to admire, expect, or uphold. What is rewarded rarely feels conditioned. It feels voluntary.

Once identity has fused with repetition, intention loses leverage. A decision made at the level of awareness struggles to compete with patterns that operate beneath it. The individual may sincerely want to act differently, but sincerity does not dismantle structure. Without altering the conditions that prepare the loop, behavior returns to its familiar form.

Understanding habits in this way reframes responsibility. Responsibility does not begin at the moment of action, when momentum is already in motion. It begins earlier—at the level of recognition. At the point where patterns become visible, where repetition is seen not as virtue or necessity, but as structure.

This recognition is unsettling. It raises questions most people never ask. If this behavior were removed, what would remain? If this pattern no longer defined me, who would I be? These questions do not arise because something is wrong, but because something has gone unquestioned.

Habits are not merely routines of behavior. They are the points where emotional momentum, cognitive framing, and social reinforcement converge. They are how internal structures sustain themselves through action. Because they are repeated, they feel stable. Because they feel stable, they feel true.

Freedom, if it is to exist at all, does not appear at the end of these loops. By then, the outcome is already determined. Freedom appears earlier, in the capacity to notice repetition before it completes itself—to recognize when behavior is being carried forward by momentum rather than chosen in the present.

This capacity is limited. It requires attention, effort, and tolerance for uncertainty. It does not eliminate habits, but it loosens their grip. It creates a margin—small, fragile, but real—within which different responses can begin to form.

Beneath habit lies another layer still—the processes that generate impulses before awareness can register them at all. To understand why behavior begins where it does, we must turn to the unconscious activity that prepares action before reflection ever enters the scene.

Chapter 6

The Unconscious Engine

Action rarely begins where we think it does. By the time a response reaches awareness, the mind and body are often already oriented toward a direction. Attention has narrowed, posture has shifted, and emotional tone has begun to organize perception. Awareness does not arrive to an empty field; it enters a process already underway.

Awareness, as it appears here, is not a separate observer standing outside the system. It is not a second self watching the first. It is a function of the same mind—one process registering the activity of another. The mind does not neatly divide into controller and controlled; it operates through feedback loops. Activity is generated, and activity is monitored. When monitoring is absent, preparation completes itself automatically. When it is present, even briefly, the system gains feedback about its own movement.

Preparation occurs through subtle but coordinated changes. Muscular tension adjusts. Breathing shifts. Attention selectively amplifies certain cues while suppressing others. Memory retrieval biases interpretation toward familiar narratives. None of this requires conscious instruction. By the time awareness registers a reaction, the body has already positioned itself toward a particular outcome.

This preparation is probabilistic, not deterministic. The unconscious engine does not command behavior; it weights possibilities. Certain actions feel more available, while others recede into the background. Choice still exists, but it exists within a narrowed field shaped by readiness rather than reflection.

This does not mean awareness is absent.

It means it is not always first.

Beneath conscious reflection operates a set of processes that prepare behavior before it is named. These processes are not hidden in a mystical sense. They are observable in experience, especially when attention is paid to timing rather than content. An impulse is felt before it is explained. A reaction is sensed before it is justified. A direction appears before it is claimed as intention.

The unconscious engine does not operate on ideas or reasons. It operates on signals. Changes in bodily state, emotional valence, memory activation, and contextual cues are its raw material. It does not ask what something means; it registers what something resembles in relation to past experience. Its task is not understanding, but orientation.

Awareness is not separate from the system it observes; it is one process registering another. It is not a homunculus standing outside the system. It is a function of the same mind—one process registering the activity of another. The system does not divide into controller and controlled; it loops.

When a situation arises, the engine scans for similarity rather than accuracy. It asks, implicitly, whether this resembles something encountered before and which response previously reduced tension, preserved stability, or restored balance. Meaning is not constructed at this level; readiness is.

The unconscious, in this sense, is not a separate mind acting against us. It is the accumulated result of prior learning operating at speed. It integrates emotional signals, bodily states, memory, and expectation to produce readiness. Its function is efficiency. Faced with recurring situations, it prepares responses without waiting for deliberation—not because it is irrational, but because deliberation is slow.

Efficiency here does not mean speed alone. It means reliability under uncertainty. The unconscious engine evolved and developed to manage situations where analysis would be too costly or too late. It favors responses that have worked before, not because they are optimal, but because they are familiar and low-risk. In ambiguity, the known is prioritized over the novel.

This preference explains why the engine resists change. Novel responses require more energy, more attention, and greater tolerance for uncertainty. The unconscious does not oppose awareness; it conserves stability.

Much of this preparation is learned. Emotional responses that once required interpretation become immediate.

Cognitive frames that once needed explanation become assumptions. Behavioral loops that once felt chosen become default. Over time, these patterns compress into automatic readiness. The unconscious engine does not decide; it prepares.

When awareness enters, it often enters late. Not too late to notice, but too late to prevent the initial movement. This is why awareness can feel weak in moments of reaction. The body is already tense. The voice has already shifted. Attention has already locked onto a particular interpretation. Awareness registers what is happening, but finds itself negotiating with momentum.

Awareness feels late because it operates at a different speed and on different data. Conscious reflection requires symbolic representation—words, concepts, narratives. The unconscious engine operates pre-symbolically, through sensation and association. By the time experience is translated into something that can be thought about, preparatory processes have already begun.

This delay is structural, not a failure. Awareness cannot be first because it depends on what the unconscious supplies: orientation, salience, and relevance.

Yet this lateness is not absolute. Awareness does not arrive after action is complete. It arrives while action is forming. This distinction matters. Awareness may not initiate the process, but it can influence whether the process completes itself unchanged.

This is why clarity often increases when awareness remains present rather than immediately discharging the impulse. The longer awareness is sustained, the more visible the sequence becomes: the emotional surge, the interpretive narrowing, the urge toward discharge. What initially appeared as a single impulse separates into components. With separation comes leverage.

The unconscious engine prepares movement, but it does not require completion. It offers a direction, not a command. Completion occurs when preparation is discharged without interruption. When awareness holds the process in view, even briefly, the loop loosens. Regulation becomes possible not by erasing impulse, but by altering its trajectory.

This capacity varies. Fatigue, stress, habit strength, and emotional intensity all affect how much influence awareness can exert. Sometimes awareness enters too late to alter the immediate outcome. Sometimes it enters early enough to soften tone, delay response, or choose silence instead of reaction. Freedom, in this sense, is not binary. It exists on a gradient shaped by timing, clarity, and effort.

The mistake is to locate agency either at the beginning or not at all. Agency does not begin before impulse, nor does it disappear because impulse exists. It emerges within the space where awareness meets momentum. That space is narrow, unstable, and easily overwhelmed—but it is real.

Understanding the unconscious engine does not absolve responsibility. It relocates it. Responsibility shifts from commanding impulses to shaping the conditions under which impulses arise. Patterns that operate beneath awareness can be strengthened or weakened through repetition, and reshaped over time. The unconscious engine is not fixed. It is plastic, responsive to repetition and reinforcement.

Deliberation matters less at the moment of impulse, and more across time. Conscious thought has limited power in interrupting a reaction already in motion, but significant power in shaping the situations that will be encountered again. When reflection alters routines, environments, expectations, or interpretations in advance, it does not override the unconscious engine—it trains it. Repeated planning does not command future behavior; it changes what future behavior feels available. Over time, what once required effort becomes easier, what once felt automatic becomes less compelling, and what once arose without question begins to hesitate. The unconscious does not learn from intention alone. It learns from repeated outcomes. In this way, deliberation operates not as a momentary intervention, but as a slow re-weighting of probabilities across experience.

The unconscious engine updates through outcome. Responses followed by relief, stability, or reward are strengthened; those followed by unresolved tension or negative consequence weaken. This learning does not require insight. It occurs through exposure and reinforcement, often without explicit awareness.

Because of this, sustained awareness matters not as a momentary interruption, but as a repeated condition. Awareness that remains present across similar situations gradually alters what the engine prepares. Over time, readiness itself changes.

To see this clearly is unsettling. It challenges the image of the self as a sovereign initiator. But it also reveals something more workable. If awareness does not need to be first to matter, then freedom does not require control at the point of origin. It requires presence at the point of emergence.

The unconscious engine prepares action. Awareness influences whether that preparation becomes destiny—or direction. The next question, then, is not whether we are free, but how the capacity of influence becomes possible within these constraints. To answer that, we must examine the boundary where awareness begins to exert influence—and how that boundary can be expanded.

Chapter 7

The Point of Influence

Even after recognizing how much of behavior is prepared in advance, the experience of choosing does not disappear.

We still experience ourselves as deciding. We still take responsibility for outcomes. We still speak in the language of ownership: I chose this, I could have done otherwise, this is on me. These experiences persist even after we understand how emotion, cognition, habit, and unconscious preparation shape what becomes available to us in any given moment.

This persistence matters.

If choice were merely an illusion in the simple sense, explanation would dissolve it. But it does not. Understanding influence does not erase the feeling of agency. It complicates it.

What has been shown so far is not that action is forced, but that it is prepared. By the time awareness registers a reaction, orientation has already occurred. Emotional tone has shifted. Attention has narrowed. Certain responses feel more accessible than others. This preparation does not eliminate choice, but it alters the field within which choice occurs.

And yet, action does not complete itself instantly.

Between preparation and execution, there is movement without closure.

A familiar situation arises. Someone says something that lands wrong. The body tightens slightly, almost imperceptibly. Attention narrows toward a single interpretation as alternative meanings recede. Breath shifts. Posture adjusts. Words begin forming before they are consciously chosen. Awareness arrives while the response is already taking shape, entering a process that has been set in motion but not yet completed.

The system is oriented, but the response has not yet resolved into behavior. This interval is subtle and easily overlooked, because it does not announce itself as a pause. There is no clear break, no neutral space, no moment where influence disappears. The process continues without interruption.

But it does not complete itself all at once.

Orientation precedes discharge. Readiness precedes action. And in this transition—brief, unstable, and often unnoticed—the process remains open.

This openness does not resemble the freedom we usually imagine. It does not allow us to choose what arises. It does not free us from influence. It does not grant authorship at the point of origin. What it allows is narrower: the possibility of participating in how an already-prepared movement resolves.

Participation enters here, not as control, but as presence.

It does not cancel emotion, undo cognition, or dissolve habit. What it can do, at times, is remain present long enough to affect how momentum completes itself. The response may soften. The action may be delayed. A familiar pattern may hesitate instead of discharging immediately.

These differences are often small. Sometimes they are barely perceptible. And sometimes they do not occur at all. The system moves too quickly. Attention is overloaded. Momentum carries the response through without interruption.

This variability does not reflect a weakness of awareness. It reflects the limits of attention under load.

The interval in which participation is possible is not fixed. It expands and contracts depending on and external conditions. Fatigue narrows it. Emotional intensity compresses it. Strong habits shorten it. Stress accelerates discharge. Under these conditions, preparation collapses into action with little room for involvement.

At other times, the interval widens slightly. Attention lingers. The unfolding sequence becomes perceptible as a sequence rather than a single impulse. The system remains active, but not yet committed to completion. It is here—only here—that capacity of influence begins to take shape.

Influence does not exist everywhere in the process.It appears within a narrow interval—after preparation has begun, but before action completes.

This reframes responsibility.

If influence does not exist at the origin of impulse, responsibility cannot be located there either. Emotional responses, urges, and early interpretations arise without deliberation. They reflect history rather than choice. Responsibility begins later, where participation becomes possible—not in isolated moments, but across time.

Not in what arises, but in how often the system is allowed to complete itself unchanged.

Each completion reinforces preparation. Each interruption—even partial—alters it slightly. Over time, these differences accumulate. The unconscious does not learn from explanation; it learns from outcome.

What is repeatedly completed becomes more likely.

What is repeatedly held, delayed, or redirected loses dominance.

Responsibility, then, is not a matter of momentary control. It is a matter of pattern formation. It concerns the conditions under which participation occurs, the environments repeatedly inhabited, and the habits allowed to stabilize without question.

Freedom does not disappear under these constraints.

It becomes a limited capacity for influence within them.

It does not exist everywhere.

It is not equally available in all conditions.

It cannot be summoned at will.

It appears only where participation meets preparation early enough to matter.

Outside this boundary, action unfolds automatically. Inside it, influence becomes possible. The boundary is narrow, unstable, and easily missed—but it is real.

To locate this boundary honestly is not to diminish freedom. It is to understand where it actually operates.

The question that remains is not whether freedom exists, but how this capacity can be made more available—what allows participation to arise earlier, more consistently, and with greater clarity.

Awareness, then, does not create freedom on its own. It does not override the conditions that precede it. It does not erase impulse, habit, or preparation. What it offers is the possibility of contact with what is already unfolding.

This contact is fragile. It can be lost as easily as it appears. Attention drifts. Emotion intensifies. Fatigue intrudes. The system completes its movement before awareness has time to remain with it. In these moments, action feels automatic not because something has gone wrong, but because nothing interrupted the process.

At other times, awareness remains present just long enough to register more than the urge itself. Sensation is noticed as sensation. Tension is felt as tension. The narrowing of attention becomes visible while it is still happening. The impulse is experienced not only as what must be done, but as something arising within experience.

This distinction is subtle, but it matters.

When impulse is experienced only as necessity, it carries authority. When it is experienced as process, it becomes negotiable. Not eliminated, not denied, but no longer absolute. The system continues to move, but its movement is no longer invisible.

This visibility creates room.

The room is not large. It does not resemble detachment or calm. Often it appears as discomfort, hesitation, or uncertainty. The familiar ease of automatic response is replaced by friction. Something wants to complete itself, and the wanting itself becomes visible.

This friction is often mistaken for weakness or indecision. In reality, it marks the point at which automaticity has been interrupted. The system has not failed. It has slowed.

Slowing does not stop momentum. It changes its shape.

A reaction held for a moment does not disappear, but it loses immediacy. A word not spoken right away does not vanish, but it becomes optional. An action delayed even briefly is no longer inevitable in the same way. The longer this delay is sustained, the more the unfolding sequence separates into parts.

What was once experienced as a single impulse begins to reveal its components: sensation, interpretation, urge, intention. With separation comes the possibility of influence—not control over what arises, but participation in what follows.

This participation is uneven. It depends on capacity. Attention must be available. Emotional intensity must remain within a tolerable range. The system must have enough stability to hold the process open without collapsing into discharge. When these conditions are absent, participation disappears.

This is not a moral failure. It is a functional limitation.

Understanding this reframes both self-blame and self-justification. If awareness fails to intervene in a moment of overwhelm, it is not because freedom was refused. It is because the conditions that allow freedom to operate were not present. Likewise, when participation does occur, it is not a triumph of will, but the result of conditions that made it possible.

Freedom, then, is not exercised equally in all moments. It cannot be demanded. It must be supported.

Support comes not from effort alone, but from the shaping of conditions over time. Patterns that repeatedly overwhelm awareness strengthen automaticity. Patterns that repeatedly allow attention to remain present weaken it. The unconscious engine adjusts not to intention, but to outcome. It learns what tends to complete itself and what tends to be held.

This is where responsibility becomes longitudinal rather than immediate.

Responsibility does not lie in commanding impulses as they arise, but in noticing which patterns are reinforced through repetition. It lies in the environments one inhabits, the rhythms one maintains, the relationships one enters, and the conditions under which awareness is repeatedly lost or sustained.

Over time, these conditions alter what the system prepares. Emotional responses soften or intensify. Cognitive interpretations loosen or harden. Behavioral loops weaken or stabilize. The boundary at which participation becomes possible shifts.

Freedom expands not because impulse disappears, but because the interval between preparation and completion becomes more accessible.

This expansion is gradual. It is not dramatic. Often it is recognized only in hindsight: a moment where a familiar response did not fully take hold, a pause where reaction once rushed through, a choice that felt quieter but more deliberate than usual.

These moments are easy to dismiss. They do not announce themselves as freedom. They often feel uncertain rather than empowering. But they mark a real change in how the system operates.

Freedom, in this sense, is not the absence of constraint. It is the capacity to remain present within constraint long enough to influence how it resolves.

This capacity does not free us from our history. It allows us to relate to it differently.

The boundary described here is not abstract. It is the point where awareness meets momentum early enough to matter. It is a threshold approached repeatedly. Sometimes we remain on one side. Sometimes we step briefly across. What matters is not where the boundary is drawn in theory, but how often it becomes accessible in experience.

The work of freedom is not to eliminate preparation, but to meet it earlier. Not to deny impulse, but to see it forming. Not to escape conditioning, but to participate in how it expresses itself.

To understand this boundary is to understand where freedom actually lives—not as an abstract ideal, but as a lived capacity shaped by timing, attention, and care.

The question that follows is not how to control the mind, but what allows awareness to enter this boundary earlier, more reliably, and with less collapse.

That question turns the inquiry toward its final layer.

Chapter 8

Awareness As The First Break

Awareness is often treated as a solution. Something to be cultivated, sharpened, or expanded in the hope that it will dissolve the forces that shape us. But nothing in the inquiry so far supports that expectation. Awareness does not erase conditioning. It does not override emotion.

And yet, it matters.

What awareness introduces is not control, but interruption.

Up to this point, the book has traced how action is prepared: through inherited structure, emotional momentum, cognitive framing, habit, and unconscious orientation. These processes operate efficiently and largely without consultation. They do not ask whether a response is wanted; they prepare what has worked before. Awareness does not stop this preparation. It arrives within it.

But awareness changes something subtle: continuity.

When preparation unfolds without awareness, it tends toward completion. Orientation moves smoothly into discharge. Reaction becomes action without resistance. The system behaves as it has learned to behave, and the sequence closes itself quickly.

Awareness introduces the possibility that the sequence does not close immediately.

This does not happen through effort or intention. It happens through contact—the direct registering of what is unfolding. When awareness is present, the unfolding process is noticed while it is unfolding. Sensation is felt as sensation. Impulse is felt as impulse. The movement toward action is registered before it completes itself.

This registration does not dissolve the movement. It does not negate it. But it alters the conditions under which it continues.

What changes is not the force of impulse, but its authority.

An impulse that is not seen feels compulsory.

An impulse that is seen feels influential, but not absolute.

This distinction is fragile and easily lost. Awareness can flicker in and out. Attention can collapse. Emotion can overwhelm. Fatigue can close the interval entirely. In these moments, awareness contributes nothing. The sequence completes itself as it always has.

This does not mean awareness failed.

It means the conditions that allow awareness to matter were not present.

Awareness is not a power. It is a capacity that depends on timing, stability, and load. It requires enough attentional space to remain present while a process is still forming. When that space exists, awareness functions as a first break in automaticity—not by stopping the system, but by preventing immediate closure.

The break is small. Often imperceptible. Sometimes uncomfortable.

It may appear as hesitation, uncertainty, or friction. The ease of habitual response is interrupted, but nothing has replaced it yet. The system remains active, but the familiar path is no longer the only one available.

This is why awareness does not feel like freedom.

It does not arrive with relief or clarity. It often arrives as tension—the tension of holding something that usually discharges immediately. This tension is frequently misinterpreted as weakness or indecision. In reality, it marks the moment where automaticity has been disrupted.

What awareness makes possible is delay without suppression.

Delay matters because the unconscious engine updates through outcome. When a prepared response completes itself unchanged, it is reinforced. When completion is delayed, softened, or redirected, the engine receives different information. Over time, this alters what is prepared in similar situations.

Awareness does not change the system by insight.

It changes it by altering what completes.

This is why awareness cannot be reduced to a moment of realization. A single insight does little. The system adapts to patterns, not explanations. What matters is not whether awareness appears once, but whether it appears often enough to influence repetition.

Over time, repeated interruptions—even partial ones—reshape readiness itself. Emotional surges become less absolute. Interpretations loosen. Behavioral loops weaken. Not because impulse disappears, but because its completion is no longer guaranteed.

This is one of the quiet ways freedom, understood as a capacity for influence, develops.

Not as mastery, but as increased negotiability.

Freedom, in this sense, is not something awareness produces directly. Awareness creates the conditions under which freedom can grow. It does so by preventing the system from closing too quickly, too often, in the same way.

This growth is uneven and reversible. Stress can undo it. Fatigue can compress it. Strong emotion can overwhelm it. There is no permanent achievement here. Only shifting probabilities.

This may sound modest, even disappointing. But it is honest.

The book began by dismantling the fantasy of free will as sovereign choice. It does not replace that fantasy with another. It ends with a quieter understanding: that freedom survives not as independence from cause, but as participation within it.

Awareness is not freedom.

It is the condition that allows freedom to take root.

It does not free us from what shaped us.

It allows us to meet what shaped us without being carried entirely by it.

This is not liberation from necessity.

It is relationship with it.

What dissolves is the expectation that control must appear at the beginning of action. What remains is something narrower, slower, and more demanding: a freedom that operates within limits, emerges over time, and depends on care rather than control.

That freedom does not promise ease.

It does not guarantee outcomes.

It does not absolve responsibility.

It only offers this: the possibility that what moves through us does not always have to move us in the same way.

And that is enough to matter.

Afterword

If there is one thing this inquiry has made clear, it is that freedom does not arrive where we were taught to look for it.

It does not appear at the moment an impulse first arises.

It does not sit behind intention as a hidden power waiting to be activated.

It is not found by denying influence, history, emotion, or conditioning.

What we call choice is shaped long before awareness enters the scene.

What we call intention arrives after preparation has already begun.

And what we call the self is not a single author, but a convergence of forces moving at different speeds.

This does not mean that freedom is an illusion in the simple sense.

It means that freedom is misplaced.

The mistake has been to imagine freedom as origin rather than participation, as control rather than contact, as exemption from influence rather than relationship with it. When freedom is placed at the beginning of action, it disappears under scrutiny. When it is placed within the unfolding of action, it becomes visible again—narrow, fragile, conditional, but real.

Freedom does not precede the system.

It appears within it.

It appears when awareness meets momentum early enough to matter.

When preparation has not yet hardened into inevitability, and when impulse has not yet closed into action.

In those moments—brief, unstable, and easily missed—something changes. Not the impulse itself, but the way it completes. Not the force of conditioning, but the shape it takes as it moves forward.

This capacity is not constant.

It cannot be demanded.

It cannot be summoned by belief or will alone.

It depends on conditions: attention, stability, timing, and care. It expands when those conditions are supported and contracts when they are not. It is strengthened not by insight alone, but by repetition—by the quiet accumulation of moments where awareness remained present just long enough to alter the course of what would otherwise have completed automatically.

Freedom, in this sense, is not heroic.

It is not dramatic.

It does not announce itself.

Often it feels like hesitation.

Sometimes it feels like discomfort.

Sometimes it feels like doing less rather than more.

And often it is only visible in hindsight.

But over time, these moments matter. They change what the system prepares. They soften what once felt fixed. They loosen what once felt inevitable. The unconscious does not need to be defeated; it needs to be met earlier, more often, and under conditions where awareness can remain present without being overwhelmed.

This is not a promise of mastery.

It is a recognition of limits.

And within those limits, something quieter becomes possible: not freedom from influence, but freedom within it; not control over what arises, but participation in how it resolves.

The question, then, is no longer whether we are free.

It is how often we are present at the boundary where freedom can occur—and what we do, repeatedly, to make that boundary more accessible.

Nothing more needs to be added here.

The rest is lived.

Appendix

On Determinism, Awareness, and Responsibility

This book has approached the question of free will indirectly—through lived experience, cognitive architecture, and temporal sequencing—rather than through exhaustive engagement with philosophical schools. This choice was intentional. Still, a brief clarification of scope and relation to existing debates may be useful.

On Neural Preparation and Libet's Experiments

The discussion of unconscious preparation draws in part on Benjamin Libet's experiments, which showed that neural activity associated with action begins before conscious awareness of intention. These findings are often interpreted as evidence that the brain "decides" before the self becomes aware.

This book does not rely on that stronger claim.

More recent interpretations, including work by Aaron Schurger and others, suggest that what Libet observed may reflect stochastic accumulation of neural activity rather than a fully formed decision. On this view, neural preparation represents increasing readiness, not inevitability. Awareness does not arrive after a decision has been made, but after a process has already begun.

This distinction matters. The argument presented here is not that conscious intention is irrelevant, but that it enters an unfolding sequence rather than initiating it. Freedom, if it exists, must therefore be located within that sequence rather than at its origin.

On Awareness and the "Homunculus" Problem

Throughout the book, awareness is described as capable of interrupting or altering automatic completion. This may appear to introduce a hidden observer—a "self" watching the mind from outside.

That is not the claim being made.

Awareness, as used here, refers to a functional capacity within the same system: a form of metacognitive monitoring in which one set of processes registers the activity of another. It is not a separate agent, nor a controller standing above the system. It is feedback, not command.

When awareness is absent, preparation tends to complete itself automatically. When awareness is present, the system gains information about its own movement. This information does not stop the process, but it can alter how it resolves. The resulting influence is real but limited, conditional, and dependent on timing.

On Deliberation and Longitudinal Responsibility

The emphasis on unconscious preparation and automaticity should not be read as a denial of deliberation, planning, or reasoned agency. Rather, it relocates their effectiveness.

Deliberation has limited power at the moment of impulse, but substantial power across time. Reflection can shape environments, habits, interpretations, and expectations in advance, thereby altering what future situations prepare. In this sense, responsibility is not exercised primarily through momentary control, but through the repeated shaping of conditions under which action unfolds.

This view aligns with reasons-responsive and compatibilist accounts of agency, while grounding them in the constraints revealed by psychology and neuroscience. The question is not whether reasons matter, but when and how they can exert influence.

On the Scope of the Argument

This book does not claim to resolve all philosophical questions surrounding moral responsibility, social freedom, or political agency. Its focus is narrower: to describe where freedom becomes functionally available within the internal architecture of human behavior.

Other dimensions of freedom—ethical, interpersonal, and structural—remain essential. But they presuppose a capacity for participation within one's own cognitive and emotional processes. This inquiry addresses that precondition.

Notes

Chapter 1 — Before Intention

Key Sources & Influences

Primary empirical foundations

- Kahneman, D. (2011). Thinking, Fast and Slow. Farrar, Straus and Giroux.

- Libet, B. (1983). "Time of conscious intention to act in relation to onset of cerebral activity." Brain, 106, 623–642.

- Kahneman, D., & Tversky, A. (1979). "Prospect Theory: An Analysis of Decision Under Risk." Econometrica, 47(2), 263–292.

- Baumeister, R. F., Bratslavsky, E., Muraven, M., & Tice, D. M. (1998). "Ego depletion: Is the active self a limited resource?" Journal of Personality and Social Psychology, 74(5), 1252–1265.

Conceptual and theoretical frameworks

- Zajonc, R. B. (1980). "Feeling and thinking: Preferences need no inferences." American

Psychologist, 35(2), 151–175.

- Schurger, A., Sitt, J. D., & Dehaene, S. (2012). "An accumulator model for spontaneous neural activity prior to self-initiated movement." Proceedings of the National Academy of Sciences, 109(42), E2904–E2913.

Related and popular interpretations

- Gladwell, M. (2005). Blink: The Power of Thinking Without Thinking. Little, Brown.

Chapter 2 — The Inherited Mind

Key Sources & Influences

Primary developmental and biological foundations

- Thomas, A., & Chess, S. (1977). Temperament and Development. Brunner/Mazel.

- Kagan, J. (1984). The Nature of the Child. Basic Books.

- Sapolsky, R. (2017). Behave. Penguin Press.

Attachment, learning, and social inheritance

- Bowlby, J. (1969). Attachment and Loss. Basic Books.

- Ainsworth, M. D. S., et al. (1978). Patterns of Attachment. Lawrence Erlbaum.

- Bandura, A. (1977). Social Learning Theory. Prentice Hall.

Identity, culture, and moral intuition

- Cooley, C. H. (1902). Human Nature and the Social Order. Scribner's.

- Gergen, K. J. (1971). The Concept of the Self. Holt, Rinehart and Winston.

- Haidt, J. (2012). The Righteous Mind. Pantheon Books.

Neurobiological continuity and momentum

- Damasio, A. (1994). Descartes' Error. Putnam.

Chapter 3 — Emotional Momentum

Key Sources & Influences

Emotional processing and neural pathways

- LeDoux, J. (1996). The Emotional Brain. Simon & Schuster.

- Damasio, A. (1994). Descartes' Error. Putnam.

Affective primacy and pre-conscious evaluation

- Zajonc, R. B. (1980). "Feeling and thinking: Preferences need no inferences." American Psychologist, 35(2), 151–175.

Dual-process and interpretive sequencing

- Kahneman, D. (2011). Thinking, Fast and Slow. Farrar, Straus and Giroux.

Constructionist and predictive models of emotion

- Barrett, L. F. (2017). How Emotions Are Made. Houghton Mifflin Harcourt.

Developmental shaping of emotional response

- Bowlby, J. (1969). Attachment and Loss. Basic Books.

- Ainsworth, M. D. S., et al. (1978). Patterns of Attachment. Lawrence Erlbaum.

Chapter 4 — Cognitive Framing

Key Sources & Influences

Attention, filtering, and perceptual selection

- Broadbent, D. E. (1958). Perception and Communication. Pergamon Press.

- Posner, M. I. (1980). "Orienting of Attention." Quarterly Journal of Experimental Psychology.

- Bar, M. (2007). "The proactive brain." Trends in Cognitive Sciences, 11(7), 280–289.

Heuristics, biases, and cognitive efficiency

- Kahneman, D. (2011). Thinking, Fast and Slow. Farrar, Straus and Giroux.
- Tversky, A., & Kahneman, D. (1974). "Judgment under Uncertainty: Heuristics and Biases." Science, 185, 1124–1131.
- Anderson, J. R. (1990). The Adaptive Character of Thought. Erlbaum.

Interpretation, schemas, and meaning formation

- Bruner, J. (1957). "On Perceptual Readiness." Psychological Review.
- Neisser, U. (1976). Cognition and Reality. Freeman.
- Fuster, J. M. (2003). Cortex and Mind. Oxford University Press.

Predictive processing and expectation

- Friston, K. (2010). "The Free-Energy Principle." Nature Reviews Neuroscience, 11, 127–138.

- Clark, A. (2013). “Whatever Next? Predictive Brains.” Behavioral and Brain Sciences, 36(3), 181–204.

Belief stabilization, identity, and motivated reasoning

- Festinger, L. (1957). A Theory of Cognitive Dissonance. Stanford University Press.
- Kunda, Z. (1990). “The Case for Motivated Reasoning.” Psychological Bulletin.
- Nisbett, R. E., & Wilson, T. D. (1977). “Telling More Than We Can Know.” Psychological Review.
- Haidt, J. (2001). “The Emotional Dog and Its Rational Tail.” Psychological Review.
- Wilson, T. D. (2002). Strangers to Ourselves. Harvard University Press.

Philosophical grounding of constrained freedom

- Spinoza, B. (1677). Ethics.

- Frankfurt, H. G. (1971). "Freedom of the Will and the Concept of a Person." Journal of Philosophy.

Chapter 5 — Habits & Behavioural Loops

Key Sources & Influences

Habit formation and automaticity

- Kahneman, D. (2011). Thinking, Fast and Slow. Farrar, Straus and Giroux.

- Wood, W., & Neal, D. T. (2007). "A New Look at Habits and the Habit–Goal Interface." Psychological Review, 114(4), 843–863.

- Bargh, J. A., & Chartrand, T. L. (1999). "The Unbearable Automaticity of Being." American Psychologist, 54(7), 462–479.

Reinforcement, loops, and behavioral stabilization

- Duhigg, C. (2012). The Power of Habit. Random House.

- Baumeister, R. F., & Vohs, K. D. (2007). "Self-Regulation and Motivation." Social and Personality

Psychology Compass.

- Baumeister, R. F., et al. (1998). “Ego Depletion.” Journal of Personality and Social Psychology.

Identity, social reinforcement, and internalization

- Cooley, C. H. (1902). Human Nature and the Social Order.
- Bourdieu, P. (1977). Outline of a Theory of Practice. Cambridge University Press.
- Bandura, A. (1977). Social Learning Theory. Prentice Hall.
- Haidt, J. (2012). The Righteous Mind. Pantheon.

Agency, responsibility, and early interruption

- Sapolsky, R. (2017). Behave. Penguin Press.
- Damasio, A. (1994). Descartes’ Error. Putnam.

- Libet, B. (1983). "Time of conscious intention to act..." Brain, 106, 623–642.

Chapter 6 — The Unconscious Engine

Key Sources & Influences

Neural preparation and preconscious action

- Libet, B. (1983). "Time of conscious intention to act in relation to onset of cerebral activity." Brain, 106, 623–642.
- Soon, C. S., Brass, M., Heinze, H. J., & Haynes, J. D. (2008). "Unconscious Determinants of Free Decisions." Nature Neuroscience, 11, 543–545.
- Dehaene, S. (2014). Consciousness and the Brain. Viking.

Emotion, bodily signals, and readiness

- Damasio, A. (1994). Descartes' Error. Putnam.
- Damasio, A. (1999). The Feeling of What Happens. Harcourt.

- LeDoux, J. (1996). The Emotional Brain. Simon & Schuster.

- Zajonc, R. B. (1980). “Feeling and Thinking.” American Psychologist.

Automaticity, heuristics, and efficiency

- Kahneman, D. (2011). Thinking, Fast and Slow. Farrar, Straus and Giroux.

- Gigerenzer, G. (2007). Gut Feelings. Viking.

- Bargh, J. A., & Chartrand, T. L. (1999). American Psychologist.

Plasticity, reinforcement, and learning

- Hebb, D. O. (1949). The Organization of Behavior. Wiley.

- Thorndike, E. L. (1911). Animal Intelligence. Macmillan.

- Schultz, W. (1998). “Predictive Reward Signal of Dopamine Neurons.” Journal of Neurophysiology.
- Daw, N. D., Niv, Y., & Dayan, P. (2005). Nature Neuroscience, 8(12), 1704–1711.
- Doidge, N. (2007). The Brain That Changes Itself. Viking.

Metacognition, feedback, and internal monitoring

- Fleming, S. M., & Dolan, R. J. (2012). “The Neural Basis of Metacognitive Ability.” Philosophical Transactions B.
- Friston, K. (2010). “The Free-Energy Principle.” Nature Reviews Neuroscience.
- Davidson, R. J., & McEwen, B. S. (2012). Nature Neuroscience.

Philosophical framing of agency

- Frankfurt, H. G. (1971). “Freedom of the Will and the Concept of a Person.” Journal of Philosophy.

- Spinoza, B. (1677/2001). Ethics. Penguin Classics.

- Sapolsky, R. (2017). Behave. Penguin Press.

Chapter 7 — The Point of Influence

Key Sources & Influences

Timing of awareness and neural preparation

- Libet, B. (1983). "Time of conscious intention to act in relation to onset of cerebral activity." Brain, 106(3), 623–642.

- Haggard, P. (2008). "Human volition: Towards a neuroscience of will." Nature Reviews Neuroscience, 9, 934–946.

- Soon, C. S., Brass, M., Heinze, H. J., & Haynes, J. D. (2008). "Unconscious determinants of free decisions in the human brain." Nature Neuroscience, 11(5), 543–545.

- Wegner, D. M. (2002). The Illusion of Conscious Will. MIT Press.

Preparation, delay, and incomplete closure

- Gollwitzer, P. M., & Sheeran, P. (2006). "Implementation intentions and goal achievement." Advances in Experimental Social Psychology, 38, 69–119.

- Friston, K. (2010). "The free-energy principle." Nature Reviews Neuroscience, 11, 127–138.

Attention limits, fatigue, and variability of control

- Baumeister, R. F., Muraven, M., & Tice, D. M. (2000). "Ego depletion: A limited resource model of self-control." Journal of Personality and Social Psychology, 74(5), 1252–1265.

- Kahneman, D. (2011). Thinking, Fast and Slow. Farrar, Straus and Giroux.

Learning through outcome and repetition

- Thorndike, E. L. (1911). Animal Intelligence. Macmillan.

- Schultz, W., Dayan, P., & Montague, P. R. (1997). "A neural substrate of prediction and reward." Science, 275(5306), 1593–1599.

- Hebb, D. O. (1949). The Organization of Behavior. Wiley.

- Wood, W., & Neal, D. T. (2007). "A new look at habits." Psychological Review, 114(4), 843–863.

Responsibility, agency, and longitudinal freedom

- Frankfurt, H. G. (1971). "Freedom of the will and the concept of a person." Journal of Philosophy, 68(1), 5–20.

- Dennett, D. C. (2003). Freedom Evolves. Viking.

Phenomenology, embodiment, and regulation

- Damasio, A. (1994). Descartes' Error. Putnam.

- Varela, F. J., Thompson, E., & Rosch, E. (1991). The Embodied Mind. MIT Press.

- Gross, J. J. (1998). "The emerging field of emotion regulation." Review of General Psychology, 2(3), 271–299.

- Ochsner, K. N., & Gross, J. J. (2005). "The cognitive control of emotion." Trends in Cognitive Sciences, 9(5), 242–249.

Philosophical foundations of gradual freedom

- James, W. (1890). The Principles of Psychology.

- Merleau-Ponty, M. (1945). Phenomenology of Perception.

- Gollwitzer, P. M. (1999). "Implementation intentions." American Psychologist, 54(7), 493–503.

- Baumeister, R. F., & Vohs, K. D. (2007). "Self-regulation and motivation." Social and Personality Psychology Compass.

Chapter 8 — Awareness as the First Break

Key Sources & Influences

Awareness timing and action formation

- Libet, B. (1983). "Time of conscious intention to act in relation to onset of cerebral activity." Brain, 106, 623–642.

- Soon, C. S., Brass, M., Heinze, H. J., & Haynes, J. D. (2008). "Unconscious determinants of free decisions." Nature Neuroscience, 11, 543–545.

- Wegner, D. M. (2002). The Illusion of Conscious Will. MIT Press.

Self-regulation through delay and inhibition

- Baumeister, R. F., & Vohs, K. D. (2007). "Self-regulation, ego depletion, and motivation." Social and Personality Psychology Compass.

- Mischel, W. (1974). "Processes in delay of gratification." Advances in Experimental Social Psychology.

Plasticity, repetition, and conditioning

- Davidson, R. J., & McEwen, B. S. (2012). "Social influences on neuroplasticity." Nature Neuroscience.

- Thorndike, E. L. (1911). Animal Intelligence. Macmillan.

- Schultz, W. (1998). "Predictive reward signal of dopamine neurons." Journal of Neurophysiology.

Probabilistic behavior and embodied cognition

- Sapolsky, R. (2017). Behave. Penguin Press.

- Damasio, A. (1994). Descartes' Error. Putnam.

Acknowledgements

This book was written in solitude, but not in isolation.

I am grateful to those who read early drafts and offered thoughtful resistance rather than easy agreement. Their questions sharpened the inquiry more than affirmation ever could.

I am thankful to the people whose conversations—sometimes brief, sometimes unfinished—forced me to clarify what I thought I understood.

And I owe quiet gratitude to those who gave me the space to write without asking what it would become.

Author Bio

Koushik Gaja is the author of Pause: What Happens Between Impulse and Action, a reflective exploration of agency, habit, and awareness grounded in psychology and lived experience.

www.ingramcontent.com/pod-product-compliance
Ingram Content Group UK Ltd.
Pitfield, Milton Keynes, MK11 3LW, UK
UKHW021409190726
13845UKWH00028B/984

9 789356 354753